Dehydrator Cookbook

Top 100 Dehydrator Recipes for Jerky, Fruit Leather, Snacks, and Tasty, Healthy, Dehydrated Meals

By: Jennifer Dolly

DEHYDRATOR COOKBOOK

Legal notice

Table of Contents

DEHYDRATOR COOKBOOK

Introduction

Put simply, food dehydration is the process of drying food to the point where the water content has been extracted. You may think that dehydrators are too expensive, but compared to the benefits they can give you, it is a relatively small investment. Besides saving the money you usually spend on wasting food, here are some of the other significant perks that a dehydrator can bring to you and your family:

- Once all the water has been removed from the food, something amazing happens to the flavor. The flavor gets intense! A thin slice of dehydrated peach, for instance, contains a huge amount of flavor which you are unlikely to find in a fresh slice. However, bear in mind that dehydrated foods are usually high in calories, so even though the flavors tempt you to eat more and more, try not to go wild.
- Dehydrated food is considered a healthy snack, as it doesn't lose its nutritional value.
- The dehydration process is simple. A very basic dehydrator can do an excellent job.
- Dehydrated food doesn't take a lot of space, which makes it portable and easy to store. You can refrigerate it and keep it for several months.

How do you dehydrate food?

The answer to this question is very simple. You just have to make up your mind and decide what you want to dehydrate, gather the ingredients, and well, leave your dehydrator to do the whole thing. Yes, it is that simple! Once you place the ingredients on the dehydrator trays and set the temperature, you won't have much to worry about except for checking when your food is ready.

When it comes to foods that can be dehydrated, you have so many options because you can dehydrate almost any type of food including:

- *Meat:* beef, fish, chicken, turkey, pork, lamb, venison.
- *Vegetables and fruits:* All types of vegetables and fruits can be dehydrated. However, some of these, such as raisins, apricots, peaches, blueberries, and Brussels sprouts, should be parboiled first in order to get better results when dehydrating them.
- *Herbs & Spices:* Chilies, ginger, garlic, lavender, onions, rosemary, stevia, and spearmint.
- Moreover, you can also dehydrate things like cheese, broth, bread crumbs, eggs, kimchi, marshmallow, milk, mushrooms, nuts, oatmeal, rice, tea, and whole grains.

What should I consider when purchasing a food dehydrator?

It entirely depends on your needs. However, having some knowledge about different types of dehydrators can help you find a perfect one for you. Some of the factors that need to be considered are below:

Ease of use: Every dehydrator is fairly simple to use; however, there are a few of them which require you to switch the shelves so that they can evenly dehydrate the food. On the other hand, some are so simple that you will just have to place the food inside, walk away, and only check when it's done.

Heat distribution & air flow: The biggest challenge for a dehydrator is to keep the heat even and consistent. Some foods will require a particular heat and air flow setup. It is advised to buy a model which ensures that the food content gets even heat and air flow until it's done. Horizontal designed dehydrators are designed best for such purpose.

Price: The price for household dehydrators ranges from $30 to over $250. The pricey dehydrators will come with a large capacity so that you can dehydrate a lot of food at once. They have impressive heat and air flow distribution, so everything is evenly cooked. They are usually coupled with little perks like thermometers and timers, which makes the complete process as simple as possible. On the lower end of the price range, there will be basic dehydrators which can accomplish drying out some foods but may not work well for all types of foods.

Timer: Dehydration takes a lot of time, so it is important to keep track of it. Sometimes, people forget about dehydrators and keep them working so that they end up with burnt food. Some models come with the timer which displays the remaining time, so you will know when your food will be ready.

Auto shutoff: It's good if your dehydrator has this feature to shutoff automatically when the food is finished. This will save energy and give you a better result.

Dehydrators will enrich your cooking experience and open up a world of opportunities. You will have a lot of healthy snacks and a lot of good-quality food to store for later use. If you have kids, dehydrated fruits, veggies, and chips are perfect healthy snacks for them. All that is left to do is enjoy the 100 recipes that follow!

CHAPTER 1: COOKIE RECIPES

Pumpkin Cookies

Calories: 85.2, Total Fat: 0.2 g, Saturated Fat: 0.0 g, Carbs: 22.2 g, Sugars: 17.4 g, Protein: 0.7 g

Serves: 4

Ingredients:
1 cup Pumpkin Puree
¼ cup Honey
¾ tsp Ground Allspice
¾ tsp Ground Nutmeg
¼ tsp Ground Cloves
¾ tsp Ground Ginger
¼ tsp Ground Cardamom
¼ tsp Ground Cinnamon

Instructions:
- Combine the ingredients and spoon onto dehydrator trays lined with parchment paper. Press with a spoon to flatten the cookies.
- Dehydrate at 145F for 12-16 hours until the desired doneness.
- Allow to cool and store in airtight containers.

Apricot Coconut Cookies

Calories: 472.1, Total Fat: 25.5 g, Saturated Fat: 3.5 g, Carbs: 61.5 g, Sugars: 43.4 g, Protein: 12.9 g

Serves: 6

Ingredients:
1 cup Unsalted Peanut Butter
2 cup Dates, pitted
1 cup Dried Apricots, soaked in warm water
1 cup Shredded Coconut
½ tsp Sea Salt

Instructions:
- Add the apricots and dates to your food processor and pulse until finely chopped. Add the peanut butter and salt and process to combine into dough. If the mixture is too dry, add in a little water.
- Roll the mixture into balls and flatten them into ¼-inch thick cookies. Arrange the cookies on dehydrator trays and dehydrate at 150F for 6-8 hours or until crisp.
- Allow to cool and store in airtight containers.

Simple Dehydrated Cookies

*Calories: 380.3, Total Fat: 9.5 g, Saturated Fat: 1.4 g,
Carbs: 69.0 g, Sugars: 11.0 g, Protein: 14.2 g*

Serves: 8

Ingredients:
2 Apples, peeled and chopped
1/2 cup Almonds
1 tsp Ground Cinnamon
4 Tbsp Flax Seeds
1/2 cup Dates
4 cup Oats
Lemon Juice, as needed, optional

Instructions:
- Add all the ingredients except the oats to your food processor or blender and puree until smooth.
- Transfer to a bowl, add the oats and mix well to combine. If the mixture is too dry, add a little water or lemon juice.
- Use the mixture to make ¼-inch thick cookies and arrange them on the dehydrator trays.
- Dehydrate for 4 hours at 113F / 45C. Flip the cookies and dehydrate for 2 more hours.
- When done, allow to cool and store in airtight containers.

Pumpkin Spice Cookies

Calories: 442.9, Total Fat: 24.1 g, Saturated Fat: 6.7 g, Carbs: 42.1 g, Sugars: 5.3 g, Protein: 20.7 g

Serves: 6

Ingredients for the cookies:
2 cups Almond Flour
2 cups Coconut Flour
2 cups Chopped Raw Pumpkin
1 cup Dates, pitted and soaked in warm water
1 3/4 cup Ground Flax Seeds
1 tsp Coconut Nectar
2 tsp Minced Ginger
1 tsp Vanilla Paste
1/4 tsp Nutmeg
2 Tbsp Cinnamon
1/4 tsp Cloves
1/4 tsp Sea Salt

Ingredients for the icing:
1 cup Desiccated Coconut
1 cup Cashews
1/2 cup Coconut Oil
Vanilla Paste, to taste
Salt, to taste

Instructions:

To prepare the cookies:

- Combine the almond and coconut flour in a large bowl and set aside.
- Add the remaining ingredients to your blender or food processor and blend until combined and smooth.
- Transfer to the bowl with the flours and mix well until dough is formed.
- Use the mixture to form cookies and arrange them on the dehydrator trays.
- Dehydrate for 4 hours at 155F / 68C. Reduce the temperature to 108F / 42C and dehydrate the cookies until the desired doneness.
- When done, allow the cookies to cool.
To prepare the icing:
- Add the ingredients to your blender or the food processor and pulse until smooth. Pour over the cookies and place in the fridge until the icing sets.

Lemon Cookies

Calories: 371.6, Total Fat: 20.6 g, Saturated Fat: 6.7 g, Carbs: 46.9 g, Sugars: 23.1 g, Protein: 6.4 g

Serves: 4

Ingredients:
1 cup Cashews
1 cup Unsweetened Dried Coconut
1 Tbsp Maple Syrup
3 Tbsp Lemon Juice

Instructions:
- Add the cashews to your blender and blend until ground. Add the coconut and pulse a few times to combine.
- Add the remaining ingredients and blend until the mixture has turned into dough.
- Use the mixture to form cookies. Arrange them on the dehydrator trays lined with parchment paper. Dehydrate for 8 hours at 150F / 65C.
- When done, allow to cool and store in airtight contains.

CHAPTER 2: CRACKER RECIPES

Carrot Crackers

Calories: 31.2, Total Fat: 0.2 g, Saturated Fat: 0.0 g, Carbs: 7.1 g, Sugars: 2.5 g, Protein: 0.9 g

Serves: 6

Ingredients:
1/2 cup Flax Seeds
1 cup Water
1 Tbsp Lemon Juice
2 Tomatoes, chopped
1/2 tsp Sea Salt
3 cup Carrot Pulp

Instructions:
- Add the flax seeds to a bowl, pour in the water and leave to soak for 4 hours.
- Add the lemon juice, tomatoes, and salt to your blender and blend until pureed. Transfer to the bowl with the flax seeds and water. Add the carrot pulp and stir well to combine.
- Line dehydrator trays with parchment paper and drop 1 tablespoon of the carrot mixture to the trays. Press with a spoon to shape the balls into crackers.
- Dehydrate at 105F / 40C for about 10 hours. Take out the crackers, remove the parchment paper, flip the crackers and continue dehydrating for 6 more hours.
- Allow to cool and store in airtight containers.

Spicy Salsa Crackers

Calories: 145.0, Total Fat: 5.5 g, Saturated Fat: 0.4 g, Carbs: 20.2 g, Sugars: 2.5 g, Protein: 4.9 g

Serves: 8

Ingredients:
1 cup Dried Quinoa, soaked in 3 cups water for 48 hours, drained
1 Tbsp Sesame Oil
1/4 cup Water
8 Garlic Cloves
1 Jalapeno
1/2 cup Corn Kernels
1 Lime, zest and juice
2 cup Pearl Tomatoes
1/2 Yellow Onion
1/4 cup Fresh Cilantro Leaves
2 Tbsp Chia Seeds, finely ground
1/2 cup Sunflower Seeds
1 tsp Himalayan salt

Instructions:
- Add the quinoa to your food processor or blender, water, and sesame oil and pulse to combine into a paste. Transfer to a bowl and set aside.
- Add the jalapeno, garlic, lime juice and zest, and corn to the food processor or blender and process until smooth. Transfer to the bowl with the quinoa mix.

- Add the onion, tomatoes, and cilantro leaves to the food processor or the blender, finely chop and transfer to the bowl.
- Add the sunflower and chia seeds, season with the salt and stir well to combine. Allow to sit for 15 minutes.
- Spread the batter onto a solid dehydrator tray and dehydrate at 115F / 46C for 5 hours. Place in a sealable container and keep in the fridge overnight.
- Take out the dough from the fridge and roll it out into a ¼-inch thick rectangle. Cut the dough into crackers, arrange them on the solid dehydrator trays. Dehydrate at 115F / 46C for 5 hours.
- Transfer to the mash tray and dehydrate for 9 more hours, flipping every 3 hours.
- Allow to cool and store in airtight containers.

Habanero Crackers

Calories: 593.4, Total Fat: 49.4 g, Saturated Fat: 6.2 g, Carbs: 28.0 g, Sugars: 4.0 g, Protein: 19.2 g

Servings: 4

Ingredients:
1 cup Raw Sunflower Seeds, soaked overnight
1 cup Cashews, soaked overnight
1 cup Raw Almonds, soaked overnight
1 Tomato, chopped into 1/4-inch pieces
1 Red Bell Pepper, chopped into ¼-inch pieces
1/4 cup Ground Flax Seeds
2 Habanero Peppers, chopped into ¼-inch pieces
A pinch of Ground Cumin
1 tsp Himalayan Salt

Instructions:
- Add the ingredients to your food processor or blender and pulse until smooth.
- Spread the puree over your dehydrator trays lined with parchment paper.
- Score the batter into crackers and dehydrate at 115F / 46C for 6-10 hours.
- Allow to cool, break into crackers and store in airtight containers.

Cheesy Kale Crackers

Calories: 469.5, Total Fat: 30.2 g, Saturated Fat: 4.9 g, Carbs: 34.7 g, Sugars: 3.9 g, Protein: 21.7 g

Serves: 6

Ingredients:
2 cup Almonds, soaked overnight, drained and rinsed
1 cup Coconut Flour
3/4 cup Nutritional Yeast
1 tsp Chipotle
1 tsp Smoked Paprika
1 bunch Kale, chopped
1 cup Ground Flax Seeds, soaked in 1 cup water
Himalayan Salt, to taste
Black Pepper, to taste

Instructions:
- Add the almonds to your blender or food processor and pulse until chopped. Transfer to a bowl and add the coconut flour, nutritional yeast, chipotle, and smoked paprika.
- Mix well to combine and add the chopped kale. Toss to combine and pour in the flax seeds together with the soaking water and season with salt and pepper. Stir well to combine the ingredients and spread (approx. ¼-inch thick layers) on a dehydrator sheet lined with parchment paper.
- Score the batter into squares or rectangles and dehydrate at 145F / 62C for half an hour. Reduce

the temperature to 118F / 47C and dehydrate for 8 more hours or until the desired doneness.

- Allow to cool and store in airtight containers.

Granola Bar Crackers

Calories: 508.2, Total Fat: 42.3 g, Saturated Fat: 16.0 g, Carbs: 31.6 g, Sugars: 20.7 g, Protein: 9.3 g

Serves: 4

Ingredients:
1 cup Ground Flax Seeds
A pinch of Cardamom
1/2 tsp Cinnamon
1/4 cup Unsweetened Cacao Nibs
1/2 tsp Orange Zest
A pinch of Salt
1-inch Fresh Ginger Root, peeled and chopped
1 cup Raw Walnuts, soaked overnight, rinsed and drained
1 large Apple, cored and chopped
1/4 cup Unsweetened Coconut Flakes, soaked in warm water for an hour and drained
1 cup Water
1/4 cup Coconut Oil
1/4 cup Agave Nectar

Instructions:
- Combine the flaxseed meal, cardamom, cinnamon, orange zest, cacao nibs, and salt and set aside.
- Add the ginger, walnuts, and apple to your food processor or blender and pulse until pureed. Transfer to the bowl with the flaxseed mixture along with the remaining ingredients. Mix well to combine the ingredients.

- Line a dehydrator tray with a non-stick sheet and pour the dough over it. Cover with another non-stick sheet, gently roll out until it is ¼-inch thick, and score it into squares or rectangles.
- Remove the top non-stick sheet and dehydrate for half an hour at 145F / 62C. Reduce the temperature to 115F / 46C and dry for 24 hours.
- When done, allow to cool, break into pieces and store in airtight containers.

Easy Raw Crackers

Calories: 234.4, Total Fat: 17.4 g, Saturated Fat: 2.2 g, Carbs: 11.7 g, Sugars: 0.1 g, Protein: 8.8 g

Serves: 4

Ingredients:
2/3 cup Whole Flax Seeds
2 cup Ground Flax Seeds
1/2 cup Sesame Seeds
1 1/3 cup Sunflower Seeds
2 2/3 cup Water
1 tsp Oregano
1 tsp Sea Salt

Instructions:
- Add the ingredients into a bowl and mix well to combine.
- Line two dehydrator trays with parchment paper and pour the batter onto the trays spreading it evenly until it is about ¼-inch thick.
- Dehydrate at 120F / 48C for an hour and then gently score the batter. Reduce the temperature to 105F / 40C and dehydrate for 6 more hours. Flip the crackers, remove the parchment paper and continue dehydrating until the desired doneness.
- When done, break into pieces and store in airtight containers.

Flax Crackers

Calories: 394.7, Total Fat: 35.3 g, Saturated Fat: 3.2 g, Carbs: 15.0 g, Sugars: 2.2 g, Protein: 11.1 g

Serves: 6

Ingredients:
1 cup Pecans
1 cup Almonds
1 cup Sunflower Seeds
1 cup Chopped Onion
1 Tomato
3 Tbsp Flaxseed
1 1/2 tsp Sea Salt

Instructions:
- Add the ingredients to your food processor or blender and pulse until combined.
- Line two dehydrator trays with parchment paper and spread the batter onto it.
- Dehydrate at 115F / 46C for an hour and then score the batter into rectangles or squares.
- Reduce the temperature to 105F / 40C and dehydrate for 6 more hours. Flip the crackers, remove the parchment paper and leave to dehydrate until the desired doneness.
- When done, store in airtight containers.

Savory Crackers

*Calories: 232.5, Total Fat: 20.6 g, Saturated Fat: 2.0 g,
Carbs: 6.2 g, Sugars: 1.9 g, Protein: 8.8 g*

Serves: 6

Ingredients:
2 cup Walnuts
1 cup Grated Carrots
1 cup Hemp Seeds
1 Tbsp Minced Shallot
1 Tbsp Fresh Herbs
1/4 cup Water
2 Tbsp Virgin Olive Oil
1/4 cup Ground Flax Seeds

Instructions:
- Add the walnuts to your food processor or blender and process until ground.
- Add the carrots, hemp seeds, shallot, herbs, water, and oil and blend until combined.
- Transfer to a bowl and mix in the ground flax.
- Line the dehydrator with parchment paper, spread the mixture and score into squares.
- Dehydrate at 115F / 46C for 10 hours. When done, store in airtight container.

Cheese Crackers

Calories: 576.1, Total Fat: 46.3 g, Saturated Fat: 14.7 g, Carbs: 25.7 g, Sugars: 3.5 g, Protein: 22.6 g

Serves: 4

Ingredients:
1 cup Ground Flax Seeds
1/4 cup Coconut Flour
1/2 cup Nutritional Yeast
2 Carrots, peeled and cut into chunks
1 Apple, cored and cut into chunks
1 1/2 cup Almonds, soaked for 8-10 hours, rinsed and drained
1/4 cup Coconut Oil, melted
1 cup Water
1 tsp White Miso
1 Tbsp Maple Syrup

Instructions:
- Mix together the coconut flour, flax seeds, and nutritional yeast and set aside.
- Coarsely grind the almonds in your food processor and add them to the coconut flour mixture.
- Add the apple and carrots to the food processor, mash them and add to the coconut mixture.
- Mix in the remaining ingredients and set aside.
- Line the dehydrator trays with parchment paper, divide the dough between the trays, cover with parchment paper and gently roll out. Remove the

top parchment paper, score the dough into squares and dehydrate at 145F / 62C for half an hour. Reduce the temperature to 115F / 46C and dehydrate for 6-8 more hours until the desired doneness.

- When done, allow to cool and store in airtight containers.

Tomato & Flax Crackers

Calories: 194.0, Total Fat: 15.3 g, Saturated Fat: 1.5 g, Carbs: 1.7 g, Sugars: 5.3 g, Protein: 8.3 g

Serves: 8

Ingredients:
4 cups Flax Seeds
2 cups Sun-Dried Tomatoes, soaked in 1 cup warm water for 30 mins
½ cup Pecans
½ cup Fresh Parsley, minced
½ cup Fresh Basil, minced
4 Garlic Cloves, peeled and minced
1 Tbsp Italian Herbs
3 Tbsp Onion Powder
1 Tbsp Maple Syrup
A Pinch of Cayenne Powder
2 tsp Coarse Sea Salt
½ tsp Coarse Black Pepper

Instructions:
- Add the flax seeds to a large bowl, pour in 6 cups of water and leave to soak for half an hour.
- In the meantime, add the tomatoes together with the soaking liquid and pecans to your blender and blend until combined. Transfer to the bowl with the flax seeds along with the remaining ingredients. Mix well until the ingredients are combined well.

- Line dehydrator trays with parchment paper and spread 3 cups of the mixture over each of the trays. Spread the mixture evenly so that the layers are 2 inches thick and score them into squares or rectangles.
- Dehydrate at 145F / 62C for 3 hours, flip the crackers and remove the parchment paper.
- Reduce the temperature to 115F / 46C and dehydrate for 6-8 more hours until the desired doneness.
- When the crackers are done, break them into squares and store in airtight containers.

Pizza Crackers

Calories: 403.2, Total Fat: 34.2 g, Saturated Fat: 4.2 g, Carbs: 15.6 g, Sugars: 0.4 g, Protein: 10.2 g

Serves: 4

Ingredients:
1 1/2 cup Flax Seeds, soaked in 2 cups of water for about 4 hours
1/2 cup Ground Flax Seeds
1/4 cup Pumpkin Seeds, ground
1/4 cup Sunflower Seeds, ground
1/2 Onion, chopped
1/4 cup Sun-Dried Tomatoes, soaked in warm water until soft
2 Garlic Cloves, crushed
1 tsp Olive Oil
1/3 cup Raw Olives, chopped
1 tsp Tamari
1 Tbsp Spices of choice
Sea Salt, to taste
A pinch of Black Pepper

Instructions:
- Add the ingredients to your food processor and pulse until dough forms. If the dough is too thick, add a little water.
- Line dehydrator trays with parchment paper and spread the dough evenly on the trays. The layers should be ½-1-inch thick.

- Dehydrate at 115F / 46C for 6 hours. Score the dough into squares, remove the parchment paper and dehydrate for 6 more hours.
- When done, store in airtight containers.

Almond & Rosemary Crackers

Calories: 408.2, Total Fat: 35.1 g, Saturated Fat: 2.8 g, Carbs: 15.3 g, Sugars: 2.8 g, Protein: 15.0 g

Serves: 4

Ingredients:
4 Tbsp Ground Flax Seeds
4 Tbsp Nutritional Yeast
2 cup Almonds, soaked overnight and drained
3 Tbsp Chopped Fresh Rosemary
1/2 tsp Sea Salt
Black Pepper, to taste
1/2-1 cup Water

Instructions:
- Add the flax seeds, nutritional yeast, almonds, rosemary, salt, and pepper to your food processor and pulse to combine the ingredients.
- Pour in ½ cup water, pulse a few times to combine. If needed, add more water.
- Line a dehydrator tray with parchment paper and spread the mixture onto it.
- Dehydrate at 115F / 46C for 4 hours and then score the dough into squares. Dehydrate for 8 more hours, break the crackers apart and flip them. Continue to dehydrate for one more hour. When done, store in airtight containers.

CHAPTER 3: FRUIT LEATHER RECIPES

Kefir Fruit Leather

Calories: 31.3, Total Fat: 0.6 g, Saturated Fat: 0.4 g, Carbs: 5.5 g, Sugars: 4.3 g, Protein: 1.1 g

Serves: 4

Ingredients:
½ cup Kefir or Yogurt
1 cup Pureed Fruit, raspberries, apricot, plums, etc.

Instructions:
- Add the fruits and kefir or yogurt to your blender and blend until smooth. Taste the puree and if it is sweet, pour in more kefir or yogurt.
- Pour the puree onto dehydrator trays lined with parchment paper and dehydrate at 115F / 46C for 8-12 hours.
- When done, peel off, cut into strips, roll up and store in airtight containers.

Pumpkin Pie Leather

Calories: 181.2, Total Fat: 1.4 g, Saturated Fat: 0.8 g, Carbs: 42.2 g, Sugars: 37.4 g, Protein: 1.4 g

Serves: 6

Ingredients:
2 cups Pumpkin Puree
2 cups Applesauce
1 cup Coconut Milk
1/4 cup Dried Shredded Coconut, unsweetened
1/4 cup Honey
1/2 tsp Ground Nutmeg
1 tsp Ground Cinnamon
1/2 tsp Ground Allspice
2 Tbsp Finely Chopped Dried Raisins or Cranberries

Instructions:
- Combine all the ingredients and spread the mixture on fruit leather dehydrator trays greased with coconut oil.
- Dehydrate at 135F / 57C for 8-24 hours depending on the thickness of the fruit leather.
- Allow to cool, cut into strips, roll up and store in airtight containers.

Peach & Ginger Fruit Leather

Calories: 73.1, Total Fat: 0.4 g, Saturated Fat: 0.0 g, Carbs: 18.8 g, Sugars: 15.7 g, Protein: 1.2 g

Serves: 4

Ingredients:
4 cups Peaches, peeled and chopped
1 Tbsp Lemon Juice
1 tsp Grated Ginger
1 tsp Vanilla Extract
1 Tbsp Honey

Instructions:
- Add the ingredients to your food processor or blender and puree until smooth.
- Spread the mixture onto dehydrator trays lined with oiled fruit leather sheets. The layers of fruit puree should be ¼-inch thick.
- Dehydrate at 135F / 57C for 6-12 hours. Transfer the fruit leather to a piece of parchment paper, cut into strips, roll up and store in airtight containers.

Yogurt Fruit Leather

Calories: 92.2, Total Fat: 2.1 g, Saturated Fat: 1.2 g,
Carbs: 12.2 g, Sugars: 8.6 g, Protein: 6.7 g

Serves: 4

Ingredients:
1 cup Raspberries, fresh or frozen
2 cup Full-Fat Yogurt
1 tsp Vanilla Extract
1 - 2 Tbsp Honey

Instructions:
- Add the ingredients to your blender or food processor and blend until smooth.
- Line dehydrator trays with parchment paper or fruit leather sheets and spread the pureed mixture into ¼-inch thick layers.
- Dehydrate at 135F / 57C for 6-8 hours. Peel off the fruit leather, place on a piece of parchment paper and cut into strips. Roll up and store in airtight container.

Plum Fruit Leather

Calories: 272.7, Total Fat: 1.2 g, Saturated Fat: 0.1 g, Carbs: 68.7 g, Sugars: 62.2 g, Protein: 3.1 g

Serves: 8

Ingredients:
7 lb Plums, halved and pitted
¾ cup Granulated Sugar

Instructions:
- Arrange the plum halves cut side down on cookie sheets and bake for about 20 minutes checking frequently to avoid burning.
- Allow the plums to cool and then puree them with the sugar in a blender or food processor.
- Line dehydrator tray with parchment paper or fruit leather sheets. Spread the pureed plums into ¼-inch layers.
- Dehydrate at 135F / 57C for 8-10 hours. When dried, place on a piece of parchment paper, cut into strips, roll up and store in airtight containers.

Pineapple Fruit Leather

Calories: 262.5, Total Fat: 0.4 g, Saturated Fat: 0.0 g, Carbs: 68.7 g, Sugars: 63.2 g, Protein: 1.8 g

Serves: 8

Ingredients:
6 lb Canned Pineapple Chunks, drained
Cinnamon, to taste

Instructions:
- Add the pineapple chunk to your blender or food processor and pulse until smooth.
- Line dehydrator trays with fruit leather sheets and grease them lightly.
- Spread the pineapple puree onto the trays into ¼-inch thick layers and sprinkle with the cinnamon.
- Dehydrate at 130F / 54C for 9-11 hours until dry to the touch.
- Place on parchment paper, slice into strips, roll up and store in airtight containers.

Apricot Fruit Leather

Calories: 74.4, Total Fat: 0.6 g, Saturated Fat: 0.0 g,
Carbs: 17.2 g, Sugars: 14.3 g, Protein: 2.2 g

Serves: 4

Ingredients:
4 cups Apricots, washed, pitted and sliced
1 Tbsp Lemon Juice
2-3 Tbsp Agave Nectar

Instructions:
- Add the ingredients into a saucepan and cook on medium-low for 20 minutes.
- Allow to cool, transfer to your blender or food processor and pulse until smooth.
- Line your dehydrator trays with parchment paper or fruit leather sheets, grease them and spread the puree into ¼-inch layers.
- Dehydrate at 130F / 54C for 6-10 hours or until dry to the touch.
- Place on parchment paper, slice into strips, roll up and store in airtight containers.

Strawberry Habanero Fruit Leather

Calories: 147.7, Total Fat: 0.7 g, Saturated Fat: 0.0 g, Carbs: 37.3 g, Sugars: 34.2 g, Protein: 1.0 g

Serves: 4

Ingredients:
1 1/4 lb Fresh Strawberries, hulled
1/2 cup Sugar
1 Tbsp Lemon Juice
1 Habanero, seeds removed

Instructions:
- Add the ingredients to your blender or food processor and blend until smooth.
- Pour into a saucepan and simmer on medium for about 45 minutes until the mixture has thickened.
- Spread onto your dehydrator trays lined with parchment paper or fruit leather sheets. Dehydrate at 130 / 54C for 6-8 hours or until dry to the touch.
- Place on parchment paper, slice into strips, roll up and store into airtight containers.

Spiced Sweet Potato Apple Fruit Leather

Calories: 156.2, Total Fat: 0.5 g, Saturated Fat: 0.1 g, Carbs: 38.0 g, Sugars: 10.8 g, Protein: 1.9 g

Serves: 4

Ingredients:
3 Sweet Potatoes, halved
3 Apples, peeled and cored
½ tsp Cinnamon
¼ tsp Ginger Powder
A pinch of Clove
A pinch of Nutmeg

Instructions:
- Preheat your oven to 400F / 200C.
- Place the apples and potato halves into a baking dish and roast for about half an hour. Take out the apples and continue to roast the potatoes for about 20 more minutes.
- Allow to cool and then peel the potatoes.
- Add the potatoes, apples, and the remaining ingredients to your food processor or blender and process until smooth.
- Spread the puree onto dehydrator trays lined with parchment paper of fruit leather sheets. Dehydrate at 130F / 54C for 6-10 hours until dry to the touch.
- Place on parchment paper, slice into strips, roll up and store in airtight container.

Blueberry Chia Seed Fruit Roll Ups

Calories: 76.8 Total Fat: 0.1 g, Saturated Fat: 0.0 g, Carbs: 19.9 g, Sugars: 15.6 g, Protein: 0.8 g

Serves: 4

Ingredients:
2 cups Blueberries
4 Dates, pitted
2 Tbsp Chia Seeds
1/2 cup Applesauce

Instructions:
- Add the ingredients to your food processor or blender and pulse until smooth.
- Spread the puree over your dehydrator trays lined with parchment paper. The layer should be 1/8-inch thick.
- Dehydrate at 115F / 46C for 8-12 hours or until dry to the touch but still pliable.
- Place the fruit leather on parchment paper, slice into strips, roll up and store in airtight containers.

Fruity Roll-Ups

Calories: 137.9, Total Fat: 0.9 g, Saturated Fat: 0.2 g, Carbs: 35.3 g, Sugars: 25.6 g, Protein: 1.9 g

Serves: 4

Ingredients:
2 Bananas, sliced
2 Peaches, sliced
2 cup Fresh Strawberries, hulled
1 Mango, chopped
1 cup Grapes, deseeded
2 Tbsp Grass-Fed Gelatin

Instructions:
- Add the fruits to your blender and blend until completely smooth.
- Add the gelatin and blend on high for a few more seconds to incorporate.
- Place parchment paper on your dehydrator sheets and pour about a cup of the fruit puree onto the first one. Tilt the tray slowly to spread the puree until it is about ¼-inch thick. Do not make it too thin because it will be difficult to remove the puree when done. Repeat the same with the remaining puree.
- Set your dehydrator to 140F / 60C and allow to dry for 6-10 hours, depending on the thickness of the puree layers.

- Once done, transfer the puree layers to parchment paper and cut them into strips. Roll them up and store in an airtight container.

Fruity Roll-Ups 2

Calories: 41.0, Total Fat: 0 g, Saturated Fat: 0 g, Carbs: 10.9 g, Sugars: 9.7 g, Protein: 0.1 g

Serves: 4

Ingredients:
2-3 cups Fruits of choice
2-3 Tbsp Honey
2 Tbsp Lemon Juice

Instructions:
- Add the fruits to your blender and blend until smooth. Add the lemon juice and honey and pulse a few times to combine.
- Line a pan with plastic wrap and pour the pureed fruits. Spread until it is ¼-inch thick and dehydrate at 140F / 60C for up to 6 hours.
- Leave to cool when done and then remove the plastic wrap.
- Cut the leather into 1-inch strips, roll them up and store in airtight containers.

Peach & Raspberry Fruit Leather

Calories: 100.4, Total Fat: 0.8 g, Saturated Fat: 0.0 g, Carbs: 25.2 g, Sugars: 15.1 g, Protein: 1.7 g

Serves: 6

Ingredients:
10 Peaches, sliced
3 cup Raspberries
Honey, to taste

Instructions:

- Puree the peaches into your blender, add honey and transfer to a bowl.
- Spread the mixture over dehydrator trays lined with parchment paper.
- Add the raspberries to the blender and blend until smooth. Pour this mixture over and swirl into the peach mixture.
- Dehydrate at 120F / 48C for 8-10 hours.
- When done, remove from the parchment paper, cut into strips, roll them up in parchment paper and store in airtight containers.

Mango Lime Fruit Leather

Calories: 141.3, Total Fat: 0.6 g, Saturated Fat: 0.1 g, Carbs: 37.5 g, Sugars: 31.0 g, Protein: 1.2 g

Serves: 6

Ingredients:
8 Mangos, peeled and diced
2 Limes, juiced and zested
Honey, to taste

Instructions:
- Add the mangoes, lime juice and zest to your blender and blend until pureed. Mix in honey and set aside.
- Line dehydrator trays with parchment paper and spread the fruit mixture onto it.
- Dehydrate at 120F / 48C for 6-9 hours. When done, cut into strips, roll up in parchment paper and store in airtight containers.

CHAPTER 4: SWEET TREAT RECIPES

Vanilla Buckwheat Crispies

Calories: 446.2, Total Fat: 4.1 g, Saturated Fat: 0.0 g, Carbs: 101.6 g, Sugars: 35.2 g, Protein: 12.0 g

Serves: 8

Ingredients:
4 cups Buckwheat Groats, soaked overnight, strained and rinsed 2-3 times for 36 hours, drained
1 Tbsp Vanilla Extract
1½ cups Maple Syrup, or to taste
1-2 tsp Sea Salt
1½ tsp Cinnamon
½ tsp Allspice

Instructions:
- Add the ingredients to your food processor or blender and pulse until combined. The mixture should not be pureed but have a little texture.
- Spread on dehydrator trays lined with parchment paper so that the layers are ½-inch thick.
- Dehydrate at 115F / 46C for 8-12 hours. Remove the parchment paper, flip the cereal and dehydrate for a couple of more hours until crunchy.
- Allow to cool, break into pieces and store in airtight containers.

Sesame Seed Macaroon Bites

Calories: 452.0, Total Fat: 17.0 g, Saturated Fat: 7.9 g, Carbs: 49.9 g, Sugars: 41.7 g, Protein: 4.1 g

Serves: 8

Ingredients:
1/4 tsp Himalayan Salt
2 tsp Dried Orange Peel
1 tsp Dried Lemon Peel
3/4 cup Honey
1 cup Sesame Seed Butter
1 cup Sunflower Seeds
2 cup Sesame Seeds
2 cups Dried Cranberries
1 cup Desiccated Coconut

Instructions:
- Add the honey, salt, orange, and lemon peel to a saucepan and heat on low, stirring continuously, until melted. Remove from the heat and leave to cool for 10-15 minutes. Add the butter and mix well to combine.
- In a separate bowl, combine the remaining ingredients and stir in the honey and butter mixture.
- Scoop the mixture onto dehydrator trays and dehydrate at 145F / 62C until the bites are crunchy but still chewy inside.
- Allow to cool and store in airtight containers.

Apricot Coco Bars

Calories: 288.4, Total Fat: 4.3 g, Saturated Fat: 1.0 g, Carbs: 62.8 g, Sugars: 38.0 g, Protein: 4.6 g

Serves: 4

Ingredients:
3 Tbsp Cacao Powder
1/2 cup Dried Figs
1 Tbsp Chia Seeds
1 1/2 cup Dried Apricot
3 Tbsp Dried Coconut
1 cup Granola Muesli

Instructions:
- Add the ingredients to your food processor and pulse until combined.
- Transfer the batter to parchment paper, cover with another piece and roll out until the layer is ½-inch thick.
- Remove the top piece of paper, transfer the rolled out batter to a dehydrator tray and dehydrate at 125F / 52C for 12 hours.
- Allow to cool and store in airtight containers.

Fluffy Pancakes

Calories: 2076, Total Fat: 0.5 g, Saturated Fat: 0.2 g,
Carbs: 54.2 g, Sugars: 37.3 g, Protein: 2.2 g

Serves: 5

Ingredients for the pancakes:
3¾ cup Ripe Bananas, chopped

Ingredients for the filling:
1 cup Water
1 cup Dates
½ cup Meat of 1 Young Fresh Coconut
¼ tsp Vanilla Powder
Berries of choice

Instructions:
- Line a dehydrator tray with parchment paper. Scoop ¾ cup of the chopped bananas onto the tray for each pancake.
- Dehydrate at 115F / 46C for 12-18 hours depending on the desired doneness. The pancakes should be soft not crunchy.
- To prepare the filling:
- Add the ingredients to your blender and blend until combined.
- Spread the mixture onto the pancakes and serve.

Banana Bread

Calories: 296.2, Total Fat: 10.6 g, Saturated Fat: 0.8 g, Carbs: 49.7 g, Sugars: 28.1 g, Protein: 5.9 g

Serves: 6

Ingredients:
1/2 cup Chopped Pecans
1 cup Raisins
1/4 cup Sesame Seeds
5 Bananas, peeled and sliced
1/4 cup Water
1 tsp Cinnamon
1 Tbsp Vanilla
A pinch of Sea Salt
1/4 cup Dates
1 2/3 cup Roughly Chopped Carrots
1/2 cup Chia Seeds

Instructions:
- Combine the pecans, raisins, and sesame seeds and set aside.
- Add the bananas, water, cinnamon, vanilla, and salt to your blender and blend until smooth. Add the dates and carrots and pulse a few more times to combine. Add the chia seeds and blend again. If the mixture gets thick, add just a bit of water.

- Transfer the mixture to the bowl with the pecans, sesame seeds, and raisins.
- Use parchment paper to line two dehydrator trays. Spread the batter onto the trays into a ¼-inch thick layer.
- Dehydrate on 140F /60C for 2 hours, score the batter and then reduce the temperature to 105 and dehydrate for a couple of hours or until the crackers seem to hold well.
- Flip the crackers, remove the parchment paper and dehydrate until the desired doneness.
- When done, leave to cool and store in airtight containers.

Raw Granola Bars

Calories: 371.6, Total Fat: 17.8 g, Saturated Fat: 1.5 g, Carbs: 51.1 g, Sugars: 28.2 g, Protein: 10.2 g

Serves: 6

Ingredients:
1 cup Dates
1 cup Almonds
2 Tbsp Water
2 Tbsp Sesame Seeds
1/2 cup Unsweetened Shredded Coconut
1/2 cup Raisins
1/2 cup Sunflower Seeds
1/2 cup Buckwheat Groats
1/3 cup Ground Flax Seeds
2 Tbsp Honey
2 Tbsp Tahini
2 Tbsp Coconut Oil
1 Tbsp Cinnamon
1 Tbsp Vanilla Extract

Instructions:
- Add the dates, almonds, and water to your blender and blend until combined but a little chunky. Transfer to a bowl, add the remaining ingredients, and mix well to combine.
- Roll out the dough and slice it into bars.

- Line dehydrator trays with parchment paper and arrange the bars onto it. Dehydrate at 150F / 65C for about 4 hours. Reduce the temperature to 115F / 46C, flip the bars and dehydrate until the desired doneness.
- When done, allow to cool and store in airtight containers.

Raw Apple Bread

Calories: 134.3, Total Fat: 6.7 g, Saturated Fat: 0.5 g, Carbs: 18.2 g, Sugars: 13.2 g, Protein: 3.3 g

Serves: 16

Ingredients:
1 1/2 cups Almonds, ground
2 tsp Cinnamon
1 1/2 cup Dates
1/2 tsp Sea Salt
3 cup Grated Apples
1/3 cup Psyllium Husk

Instructions:
- Add the ground almonds, cinnamon, dates, and salt to your food processor and pulse until combined. Transfer to a bowl and add the grated apples and psyllium husk and mix well.
- Use the mixture to form 8 small loaves and arrange them on the dehydrator trays lined with parchment paper.
- Dehydrate at 150F / 65C for an hour. Reduce the temperature to 110F / 43C and continue dehydrating for 5 more hours.
- When done, allow to cool and store in the fridge.

Chocolate Chips

Calories: 183.8, Total Fat: 12.8 g, Saturated Fat: 0.0 g, Carbs: 19.2 g, Sugars: 0.2 g, Protein: 2.6 g

Serves: 4

Ingredients:
2 Tbsp Lucuma Powder
1/4 tsp Vanilla Bean Powder
2 Tbsp Cacao Powder
1/4 cup Raw Coconut Nectar
1/2 tsp Himalayan Salt
2 cups Large Coconut Ribbons, soaked for 4 hours and strained

Instructions:
- Combine the ingredients in a bowl, add the coconut and mix well.
- Spread the mixture on the dehydrator trays lined with parchment paper. Dehydrate at 115F / 46C for 4 hours. Remove the parchment paper, place the chips on mesh and dehydrate for 16-18 more hours.
- When done, allow to cool and store in airtight containers.

Hot Cross Buns

Calories: 361.8, Total Fat: 20.1 g, Saturated Fat: 2.9 g, Carbs: 42.9 g, Sugars: 22.3 g, Protein: 9.0 g

Serves: 8

Ingredients for the buns:
½ cup Coconut Flour
1½ cup Almond Meal
¼ cup + 2 Tbsp Coconut Sugar
¾ cup Grated Apple
¼ cup Psyllium Husks
5 Dates, pitted
¼ cup + 2 Tbsp Almond Milk
1 Tbsp Cacao Powder
1½ tsp Cinnamon Powder
1 tsp Mixed Spice
Zest of 1/2 Orange
Coarse Sea Salt, to taste
1 cup Raisins

Ingredients for the cross:
1½ cup Almond Meal
½ cup Cashews, soaked in water until soft, drained
Juice of 1/2 Lemon
2 Tbsp Coconut Oil, melted
¼ cup Water
1 Tbsp Maple Syrup
1 tsp Vanilla Extract

A pinch of Coarse Sea Salt

Instructions:

To prepare the buns:

- Add all the ingredients except the raisins to your food processor and pulse until dough forms. Transfer to a bowl and add the sultanas.
- Line a square baking tin (approx. 8-inch tin) with parchment paper and press the dough into the tin. Leave to sit for 10 minutes, remove from the tin and cut into 16 squares.
- Arrange the buns onto the dehydrator trays lined with parchment paper, brush with the maple syrup and dehydrate at 135F / 57C for an hour.
- Reduce the temperature to 115F / 46C and dehydrate for 4 to 5 more hours.
- When done, set aside to cool.
  To prepare the crosses:
- Add the ingredients to the food processor and pulse until smooth. Transfer to a piping bag and pipe crosses over the buns.
- Allow the icing to set, serve or store in airtight containers.

Strawberry Oat Bars

Calories: 400, Total Fat: 11.4 g, Saturated Fat: 2 g, Carbs: 70.6 g, Sugars: 32.0 g, Protein: 10 g

Serves: 4

Ingredients:
1/2 cup Mashed Banana
3/4 cup Dates, pitted
1/4 cup Peanut Butter
1/4 tsp Sea Salt
1 cup Dried Strawberries
3 Tbsp Chia Seeds
3 Tbsp Hemp Seeds
3 Tbsp Ground Flax Seeds
2 cups Rolled Oats

Instructions:
- Add the banana, dates, butter, and salt in your food processor and pulse until combined. Mix in the seeds and half the oats.
- Transfer to a bowl and stir in the strawberries and remaining ingredients.
- Line a dehydrator tray with parchment paper, spread the batter into a 1-inch thick square and dehydrate at 145 / 62C for 4 hours. Cut the dough into 6 bars and dehydrate at 115 / 46C for 4 more hours. Store the bars in the fridge.

CHAPTER 5: SNACK RECIPES

Chedda Onions

Calories: 164.4, Total Fat: 8.3 g, Saturated Fat: 0.9 g, Carbs: 20.0 g, Sugars: 0.4 g, Protein: 5.3 g

Serves: 8

Ingredients:
3 lb Onions, sliced into ¼-inch rounds
1 cup Sunflower Seeds, soaked for 3-6 hours
1/2 Red Pepper
2 Tbsp Nutritional Yeast
1 Tbsp Olive Oil
1 Tbsp Lemon Juice
1 Tbsp Tahini
1/2 Garlic Clove
Sea Salt, to taste

Instructions:
- Add all the ingredients except the onions to your blender and blend until smooth.
- Add the onions to a bowl, pour the sauce over and toss to coat.
- Arrange the onions on dehydrator trays lined with parchment paper and dehydrate for 24 hours at 115F / 46C or until crispy.
- Allow to cool and store in airtight containers.

Cheesy Garlic Kale

Calories: 225.7, Total Fat: 16.2 g, Saturated Fat: 2.8 g, Carbs: 17.1 g, Sugars: 2.4 g, Protein: 7.2 g

Serves: 4

Ingredients:
1 Sweet Red Pepper, deseeded
5 Garlic Cloves, smashed
1/4 cup Raw Sunflower Seeds, soaked for 4 hours and drained
3/4 cup Raw Cashews, soaked for 4 hours and drained
1/4 cup Nutritional Yeast
2 Tbsp Lemon Juice
1 tsp Sea Salt
2 Chives
2 bunches of Kale, stems removed

Instructions:
- Add all ingredients except the kale to your blender and blend until smooth.
- Pour the mixture over the kale and toss to coat.
- Arrange the kale on dehydrator trays and dehydrate at 105F / 40C for 7-15 hours until crispy.
- Allow to cool and store in airtight containers.

Almond Crumbles

Calories: 503.7, Total Fat: 36.2 g, Saturated Fat: 3.4 g, Carbs: 39.5 g, Sugars: 20.5 g, Protein: 16.6 g

Serves: 8

Ingredients:
4 cup Raw Almonds
1 Tbsp Sea Salt
3/4 cup Maple Syrup
3/4 cup Cocoa Powder
3 Tbsp Coconut Oil
1/2 cup Shredded Coconut
1 tsp Vanilla Extract

Instructions:
- Add the almonds to a large bowl, sprinkle with the salt and fill with filtered water. Leave to soak for 12-24 hours. Drain and rinse the almonds and grind in your blender or food processor until you read the desired texture. Transfer to a bowl.
- Add the remaining ingredients and mix well.
- Spread the mixture into 1-inch layers onto dehydrator trays. Dehydrate at 115F / 46C for 24 hours.
- Allow to cool to room temperature. If the crumbles are still not crunchy, dehydrate at 115F / 46C for 2-3 more hours. Store in airtight containers.

Curried Pumpkin Seeds

Calories: 142.7, Total Fat: 6.2 g, Saturated Fat: 1.1 g, Carbs: 17.2 g, Sugars: 0.1 g, Protein: 6.0 g

Serves: 2

Ingredients:
1 cup Raw Pepitas, soaked for 7 hours and drained
1 tsp Turmeric
1 tsp Sea Salt
1 tsp Minced Garlic
1 tsp Curry Powder

Instructions:
- Mix together the spices. Add the pepitas and toss to coat.
- Spread the pepitas onto dehydrator trays and dehydrate at 145F /62C until the seeds are crisp.
- Allow to cool and store in airtight containers.

Paleo Granola

Calories: 579.3, Total Fat: 42.1 g, Saturated Fat: 11.6 g, Carbs: 50.0 g, Sugars: 32.3 g, Protein: 11.6 g

Serves: 6

Ingredients:
2 cup Hazelnuts, chopped
1/2 cup Cashews
1/2 cup Pumpkin Seeds, chopped
2 Tbsp Sesame Seeds
2 Tbsp Coconut Oil, melted
1/4 cup Honey
2 Tbsp Almond Butter
1 tsp Vanilla Extract
1 tsp Cinnamon
1/4 tsp Ginger Powder
1/2 tsp Celtic Sea Salt
3/4 cup Unsweetened Coconut Flakes
1/4 cup Raw Cacao Nibs
1/2 cup Dried Cranberries or Raisins

Instructions:
- Mix together the honey, coconut oil, and butter into a paste. Stir in the cinnamon, vanilla, ginger, and salt.
- Add the nuts and seeds and stir well to coat the nuts. Sprinkle with the coconut and mix well.

- Spread on your dehydrator trays and dehydrate at 115F / 46C for 6-8 hours or until dry and crunchy.
- Add the dried fruits and cacao nibs and store in airtight containers.

Snap Pea Chips

Calories: 26.4, Total Fat: 0.2 g, Saturated Fat: 0.0 g,
Carbs: 4.9 g, Sugars: 2.5 g, Protein: 1.9 g

Serves: 4

Ingredients:
3-4 cup Snap Peas, fresh or frozen
2 -3 tsp Oil
1/2 tsp Garlic Powder
3-4 Tbsp Nutritional Yeast
1/2 tsp Sea Salt

Instructions:

- Rinse the snap peas, pat dry and arrange on parchment paper.
- Drizzle with the oil, sprinkle with the garlic powder, nutritional yeast, and salt and toss to coat.
- Arrange the snap peas on dehydrator trays and dehydrate at 135F / 57C for about 8 hours.
- Allow to cool when done and store in airtight containers.

Cauliflower Popcorn

Calories: 197.4, Total Fat: 0.9 g, Saturated Fat: 0.1 g, Carbs: 17.3 g, Sugars: 28.2 g, Protein: 6.9 g

Serves: 4

Ingredients:
2 heads of Cauliflower, separated into florets and chopped

Ingredients for the sauce:
¼ cup Sun-Dried Tomatoes, soaked in warm water for an hour
½ cup Water
3 Tbsp Nutritional Yeast
1 cup Dates
2 Tbsp Tahini
2 tsp Garlic Powder
1 Tbsp Apple Cider Vinegar
1-2 tsp Cayenne Pepper
2 tsp Onion Powder
½ tsp Turmeric

Instructions:
To prepare the sauce:
- Add the ingredients to your blender and blend until smooth and thick. Transfer to a large bowl and set aside.
- Add the chopped cauliflower and toss to coat.

- Arrange the cauliflower on dehydrator trays and dehydrate at 115F / 46C for about 12 or up to 24 hours until the desired doneness.
- Allow to cool and store in airtight containers.

Eggplant Bacon

Calories: 257.7, Total Fat: 13.9 g, Saturated Fat: 1.9 g,
Carbs: 31.9 g, Sugars: 11.7 g, Protein: 4.5 g

Serves: 4

Ingredients:
1.5 lb Eggplant, rinsed, destemed, sliced to 1/4-inch long strips
1/4 cup Olive Oil
1/4 cup Vinegar
1/4 cup Tamari
1/4 cup Maple Syrup
1 tsp Smoked Paprika
2 tsp Chili Powder
1/2 tsp Cayenne Pepper
1/2 tsp Sea Salt

Instructions:
- Place the eggplant slices in a baking dish and set aside.
- Whisk together the remaining ingredients and pour over the eggplant. Make sure that all the slices are well coated with the marinade. Leave to marinate for an hour.
- Arrange the slices on dehydrator trays, shaking off any excess and dehydrate at 140F / 60C for 12-16 hours.
- Allow to cool and store in airtight containers.

Black Bread

Calories: 324.1, Total Fat: 18.7 g, Saturated Fat: 1.5 g, Carbs: 38.4 g, Sugars: 4.6 g, Protein: 9.8 g

Serves: 4

Ingredients:
1 cup Raw Walnuts, soaked overnight, rinsed and drained
1 cup Buckwheat Groats, soaked overnight, rinsed and drained
2 Garlic Cloves, peeled
1/4 cup Water
1 tsp Lemon Juice
1/4 cup Chopped Red Onion
1 Tbsp Agave Nectar
1 Tbsp Cacao Powder
1/4 cup Ground Flax Seeds
1 Tbsp Caraway seeds
1/4 tsp Black Pepper

Instructions:
- Add the walnuts and buckwheat groats to your blender or food processor and pulse until chopped. Add the garlic, water, lemon juice, onion, and agave nectar and pulse until combined.
- Transfer to a bowl and mix in the cacao, flaxseed meal, caraway seeds, and pepper.

- Pour the dough onto a dehydrator sheet, spread it until it is ¼-inch thick and score it into squares or rectangles.
- Dehydrate at 115F / 46C for 8 to 12 depending on the preferred doneness.
- When done, break into pieces and store in airtight containers.

Raw Zucchini Bread

Calories: 373.7, Total Fat: 22.5 g, Saturated Fat: 2.0 g, Carbs: 45.9 g, Sugars: 33.8 g, Protein: 6.9 g

Serves: 6

Ingredients:
2 cup Walnuts
2 tsp Cinnamon
1 1/2 cups Dates
1 tsp Vanilla Extract
3 cup Grated Zucchini
1 cup Shredded Unsweetened Coconut
1/2 cup Raisins
1/2 cup Psyllium Husk

Instructions:
- Add the walnuts to your food processor and pulse until ground. Add the cinnamon, dates, and vanilla and process until combined.
- Transfer to a bowl, add the zucchini, coconut, raisins, and psyllium husk and mix well to combine.
- Use the mixture to make 10 loaves and place them on the dehydrator trays lined with parchment paper.
- Dehydrate at 150F / 65C for an hour, reduce the temperature to 110F / 43C and dehydrate for 5 more hours.
- When done, allow to cool and store in the fridge.

Potato Pancakes

Calories: 217.5, Total Fat: 14.1 g, Saturated Fat: 1.0 g, Carbs: 20.9 g, Sugars: 1.8 g, Protein: 4.9 g

Serves: 2

Ingredients:
1 Potato, grated
1/2 Purple Onion, chopped
1 Garlic Clove, minced
1 Tbsp Celtic Sea Salt
Water
1/3 cup Pine Nuts, finely ground
1 Tbsp Olive Oil
2 Tbsp Dried Rosemary

Instructions:
- In a bowl, combine the potato, onion, garlic, and salt, fill the bowl with water and soak for 10 minutes. Drain the mixture, add the pine nuts, olive oil, and rosemary and mix well.
- Spread the mixture onto dehydrator trays and shape them into round pancakes.
- Dehydrate at 145F for 45 minutes. Reduce the temperature to 115F and dehydrate for 2 more hours.
- Allow to cool and store in airtight containers.

CHAPTER 6: VEGETABLE RECIPES

Veggie Chips

Calories: 54.0, Total Fat: 0.2 g, Saturated Fat: 0.0 g, Carbs: 12.5 g, Sugars: 2.3 g, Protein: 1.6 g

Serves: 4

Ingredients:
1 Yellow Squash
1 Sweet Potato
1 Zucchini

Instructions:
- Slice the vegetables into ¼-inch thick rounds.
- Bring a pot with water to the boil, add the veggie slices and blanch for 5 minutes. Drain and leave to cool.
- Sprinkle the veggies with salt and arrange on dehydrator trays. Dry at 120F / 48C for 4-6 hours depending on the desired doneness.
- Allow to cool and store in airtight container.

Green Bean Crisps

*Calories: 77.5, Total Fat: 0.3 g, Saturated Fat: 0.1 g,
Carbs: 17.9 g, Sugars: 0.1 g, Protein: 4.6 g*

Serves: 4

Ingredients:
2 lb Fresh Green Beans, washed and trimmed
A pinch of Sea Salt
1 tsp Olive Oil

Instructions:
- Season the beans with salt and toss to coat.
- Arrange the beans on dehydrator trays dehydrate at 120F / 48C for 2-4 hours.
- Drizzle with the oil, allow to cool and store in airtight containers.

Sweet Potato Chips

Calories: 68.3, Total Fat: 0.2 g, Saturated Fat: 0 g, Carbs: 15.8 g, Sugars: 0.1 g, Protein: 1.1 g

Serves: 4

Ingredients:
2 Sweet Potatoes, peeled and sliced into ¼-inch rounds
Juice from 1/2 Lime
A pinch of Sea Salt

Instructions:
- Bring a pot of water to the boil. Add the potato slices and blanch for 5 minutes. Drain and leave to cool.
- Drizzle the potatoes with the lime juice, sprinkle with salt and toss to coat.
- Arrange the slices on dehydrator trays and dehydrate on 120F / 48C for 4-6 hours.
- Allow to cool and store in airtight containers.

Sun-Dried Tomatoes

Calories: 52, Total Fat: 1 g, Saturated Fat: 0.1 g, Carbs: 11.6 g, Sugars: 0 g, Protein: 2.1 g

Serves: 4

Ingredients:
2 lbs Roma Tomatoes
Sea Salt, to taste

Instructions:
- Halve the tomatoes, discard the seed, and arrange the tomato halves on dehydrator trays lined with parchment paper.
- Dehydrate on 135F / 67C for 12-18 hours depending on the desired doneness.
- Allow to cool and store in airtight containers.

Rosemary Sweet Potato Chips

Calories: 17.6, Total Fat: 13.7 g, Saturated Fat: 1.9 g, Carbs: 15.8 g, Sugars: 0.0 g, Protein: 1.1 g

Serves: 2

Ingredients:
1 Sweet Potato, sliced into paper-thin rounds
2 Tbsp Olive Oil
1 Tbsp Lemon Juice
1 tsp Dried Rosemary, crushed
1/2 tsp Sea Salt

Instructions:
- Add the potato slices into a bowl, drizzle with the lemon juice and oil and rub gently to coat.
- Sprinkle with the rosemary and salt and toss to coat.
- Arrange the potato slices on dehydrator trays and dehydrate at 115F /46C for 6-10 hours or until crispy.
- Allow to cool and store in airtight containers.

Spicy Cucumber Chips

Calories: 24.1, Total Fat: 0.3 g, Saturated Fat: 0.0 g, Carbs: 4.3 g, Sugars: 2.8 g, Protein: 1.2 g

Serves: 2

Ingredients:
2 Cucumbers, peeled and thinly sliced
1 tsp Apple Cider Vinegar
1/4 tsp Salt

Instructions:
- Mix together the vinegar and salt, drizzle the cucumbers and toss to coat.
- Arrange the cucumber slices on dehydrator trays and dehydrate at 135F /57C for 4 hours.
- Allow to cool and store in airtight containers.

Dried Jalapeno Peppers

Calories: 18.8, Total Fat: 0.4 g, Saturated Fat: 0.0 g,
Carbs: 3.7 g, Sugars: 2.2 g, Protein: 0.8 g

Serves: 8

Ingredients:
1 lb Jalapeno Peppers, rinsed

Instructions:
- Slice the peppers lengthwise, discard the seeds and pith and arrange on dehydrator trays.
- Dehydrate at 145F /62C for 8-12 hours or until completely dried.
- Allow to cool and store in airtight containers.

Parmesan Zucchini Chips

Calories: 69.8, Total Fat: 2.9 g, Saturated Fat: 1.8 g, Carbs: 6.9 g, Sugars: 2.8 g, Protein: 5.0 g

Serves: 3

Ingredients
1 lb Zucchini, thinly sliced
1/8 tsp Sea Salt
1 oz Parmesan Cheese, finely grated
1 Garlic Clove, finely grated
1 tsp Apple Cider Vinegar

Instructions:

- Place the zucchini into a bowl and sprinkle with the garlic, vinegar, cheese, and salt. Toss to coat and arrange on dehydrator trays.
- Dehydrate at 135F / 57C for 10 hour or until crispy.
- Allow to cool and store in airtight containers.

Parmesan Tomato Chips

Calories: 88.0, Total Fat: 5.8 g, Saturated Fat: 1.1 g, Carbs: 9.4 g, Sugars: 0.8 g, Protein: 2.2 g

Serves: 6

Ingredients:
6 cup Thinly Sliced Tomatoes
2 Tbsp Olive Oil
2 tsp Sea Salt
1 tsp Garlic Powder
2 Tbsp Freshly Chopped Parsley
2 Tbsp Grated Parmesan Cheese

Instructions:
- Place the tomatoes in a bowl, drizzle with the olive oil and toss to coat.
- Arrange the slices on dehydrator trays.
- Mix together the remaining ingredients and sprinkle over the tomato slices.
- Dehydrate at 115F / 46C for 12-24 hours depending on the thickness of the slices.
- Allow to cool and store in airtight containers.

Vinegar Zucchini Chips

Calories: 40, Total Fat: 3.6 g, Saturated Fat: 0.5 g, Carbs: 2.9 g, Sugars: 2.0 g, Protein: 0.7 g

Serves: 8

Ingredients:
4 cup Thinly Sliced Zucchini
2 Tbsp Olive Oil
2 Tbsp Balsamic Vinegar
2 tsp Coarse Sea Salt

Instructions:
- Drizzle the zucchini sliced with vinegar and oil and toss to coat.
- Arrange the slices on dehydrator trays and sprinkle with the salt.
- Dehydrate at 135F / 57C for 8-14 hours or until crispy.
- Allow to cool and store in airtight containers.

Beet Chips

*Calories: 11.0, Total Fat: 1.2 g, Saturated Fat: 0.2 g,
Carbs: 2.5 g, Sugars: 2.0 g, Protein: 0.4 g*

Serves: 4

Ingredients:
2 Beets, thinly sliced
1 tsp Olive Oil

Instructions:
- Drizzle the beet slices with the oil and toss to coat.
- Arrange the slices onto your dehydrator trays and dehydrate at 130F / 54C for 8-12 hours depending on the thickness of the slices.
- Allow to cool and store in airtight containers.

Brussels Sprout Chips

Calories: 50.0, Total Fat: 2.5 g, Saturated Fat: 2.0 g, Carbs: 6.4 g, Sugars: 1.6 g, Protein: 2.4 g

Serves: 4

Ingredients:
12-15 Brussels Sprouts
1 Tbsp Coconut Oil
1/2 tsp Sea Salt
1/2 tsp Black Pepper

Instructions:

- Trim the ends and peel off the outer leaves. Cut ¼-inch off the end of the sprouts and peel off more leaves.
- Place the leaves into a bowl, drizzle with the oil and season with salt and pepper. Toss to coat and arrange the leaves on your dehydrator trays lined with parchment paper.
- Dehydrate at 125F / 52C for 6-8 hours. Allow to cool and store in airtight containers.

Raw Corn Chips

Calories: 88.6, Total Fat: 1.1 g, Saturated Fat: 0.2 g, Carbs: 20.3 g, Sugars: 0.1 g, Protein: 2.9 g

Serves: 3

Ingredients:
2 cup Sweet Corn

Instructions:
- Add the corn to your food processor or blender and pulse until smooth.
- Spread over your dehydrator tray lined with parchment paper.
- Dehydrate at 115F / 46C for 4 hours. Score the batter into triangles or squares and continue dehydrating for 4-6 more hours.
- Allow to cool, break into pieces and store in airtight containers.

Sriracha Beet Chips

Calories: 31.7, Total Fat: 1.2 g, Saturated Fat: 1.0 g, Carbs: 5.0 g, Sugars: 4.0 g, Protein: 0.8 g

Serves: 8

Ingredients:
8 Beets, peeled and sliced into paper-thin slices
1-2 tsp Coconut Oil, melted
Sriracha Seasoning, to taste

Instructions:
- Drizzle the beet slices with the coconut oil, season and toss to coat.
- Arrange on your dehydrator trays and dehydrate at 120F / 50C for 6-8 hours.
- Allow to cool and store in airtight containers.

CHAPTER 7: FRUIT RECIPES

Dehydrated Raspberries

Calories: 61.3, Total Fat: 0.7 g, Saturated Fat: 0.0 g, Carbs: 14.5 g, Sugars: 0.3 g, Protein: 1.1 g

Serves: 4

Ingredients:
1 lb Fresh Raspberries

Instructions:
- Rinse the raspberries and remove any debris. Discard smashed, spongy, and deep-dark raspberries.
- Spread the raspberries on a tray and air dry to remove any moisture.
- Transfer the raspberries on your dehydrator trays.
- Set your dehydrator to 135F / 57C and leave to dry for 12 to 18 hours.
- Store in an airtight container and set aside or use immediately.

Dehydrated Lemons

*Calories: 75.0, Total Fat: 0.2 g, Saturated Fat: 0.0 g,
Carbs: 18.8 g, Sugars: 17.4 g, Protein: 1.4 g*

Serves:4

Ingredients:
2 lb Fresh Lemon

Instructions:
- Rinse the lemons well and slice them into ¼-inch thick circles.
- Discard the seeds and arrange the slices on your dehydrator trays.
- Set your dehydrator to 135F / 57C and dry for about 24 hours.
- The lemons are done once the color of the inside is changed to brown. Store in an airtight container and set aside.

Orange Chips

Calories: 117.6, Total Fat: 0.2 g, Saturated Fat: 0.0 g, Carbs: 29.4 g, Sugars: 23.7 g, Protein: 2.3 g

Serves: 4

Ingredients:
2 lb Fresh Oranges

Instructions:

- Rinse the oranges and slice them into ¼-inch thick slices.
- Arrange the slices on your dehydrator trays, set it to 135F / 57C and leave to dry for 8-12 hours.
- Once done, store in an airtight container and set aside.

Apple Chips

Calories: 87.8, Total Fat: 0.2 g, Saturated Fat: 0.0 g,
Carbs: 23.3 g, Sugars: 18.6 g, Protein: 0.3 g
Serves: 4

Ingredients:
4 Fresh, Crisp Apples
1 Tbsp Granulated Sugar
1 Tbsp Ground Cinnamon

Instructions:
- Rinse the apples and slice them into ¼-inch thick slices and discard the seeds.
- Sprinkle with the sugar and cinnamon and toss to coat evenly.
- Arrange the apple slices on your dehydrator trays, set to 135F / 57C and allow to dry for about 6 to 8 hours.
- When the apples are dried, store in an airtight container and set aside.

Dehydrated Strawberries

*Calories: 75.0, Total Fat: 1.0 g, Saturated Fat: 0.0 g,
Carbs: 17.6 g, Sugars: 13.2 g, Protein: 1.5 g*

Serves: 4

Ingredients:
2 lb Fresh Strawberries

Instructions:
- Rinse the strawberries and leave them in a colander to drain.
- Discard the hulls and any overripe berries.
- Slice the strawberries to ¼-inch thick slices and arrange them on your dehydrator trays.
- Set your dehydrator to 135F / 57C and allow the fruits to dry for 8-10 hours.
- Store the dried strawberries in an airtight container and set aside.

Dehydrated Plums

Calories: 115.0, Total Fat: 0.7 g, Saturated Fat: 0.0 g,
Carbs: 27.6 g, Sugars: 24.7 g, Protein: 1.9 g
Serves: 4

Ingredients:
2 lb Fresh Plums

Instructions:
- Rinse the plums, slice them in half around the pit and discard the pit.
- Arrange the plum halves cut side down on your dehydrator trays.
- Set to 145F / 62C and allow to dry for 4-6 hours. Check the plums every 2 hours and flip if necessary to complete drying.
- Store in an airtight container and set aside.

Dehydrated Cranberries

Calories: 115.0, Total Fat: 0.3 g, Saturated Fat: 0.0 g,
Carbs: 30.5 g, Sugars: 10.1 g, Protein: 1.0 g
Serves: 4

Ingredients:
2 lb Fresh Cranberries

Instructions:
- Rinse and halve the cranberries.
- Arrange them on the dehydrator trays and dry for about 24 hours at 100F / 38C.
- Once the cranberries are dried, store them in an airtight container and set aside.

Dehydrated Pears

Calories: 121.2, Total Fat: 0.3 g, Saturated Fat: 0.0 g, Carbs: 31.9 g, Sugars: 20.6 g, Protein: 0.9 g

Serves: 4

Ingredients:
2 lb Fresh Pears
1 cup Lemon Juice
1 gallon Water

Instructions:
- Rinse the pears, cut off any bruised spots and slice the pears into ¼-inch thick rings.
- Combine the lemon juice and water and soak the pear slices for about 10 minutes.
- Arrange the pear slices on your dehydrator trays and dry for about 3-6 hours at 160F / 70C.
- When done, store in an airtight container and set aside.

Dehydrated Pineapple

Calories: 138.9, Total Fat: 1.3 g, Saturated Fat: 0.0 g, Carbs: 35.1 g, Sugars: 29.2 g, Protein: 1.1 g

Serves: 10

Ingredients:
6 Ripe Pineapples (do not use overripe pineapples)

Instructions:
- Chop off the top and bottom parts, peel the pineapples and slice into ¼-inch thick slices.
- Arrange the slices on the dehydrator trays and dry for 12-14 hours at 135F / 57C.
- Store in airtight containers and set aside.

Dehydrated Blueberries

Calories: 140.0, Total Fat: 0.0 g, Saturated Fat: 0.0 g, Carbs: 35.3 g, Sugars: 25.9 g, Protein: 1.7 g

Serves: 4

Ingredients:
2 lb Fresh Blueberries

Instructions:
- Rinse the blueberries and set aside.
- Fill a large pot with water and bring it to the boil. Add the blueberries and blanch for half a minute or until their skins just start to crackle.
- Transfer the blueberries into a pot filled with icy cold water.
- Drain the berries and arrange on the dehydrator trays. Dehydrate at 135F / 57C for 35 hours or until dried.
- Allow to cool and store in airtight containers.

Dehydrated Grapefruit

Calories: 176.9, Total Fat: 0.1 g, Saturated Fat: 0 g, Carbs: 44 g, Sugars: 34.4 g, Protein: 2.4 g

Serves: 2

Ingredients:
2 Grapefruits

Instructions:
- Slice the grapefruits into ¼-inch thick slices.
- Arrange on the dehydrator trays and leave to dry at 135F / 57C for 8-12 hours until dried.
- Store in an airtight container and set aside.

Dehydrated Peaches

Calories: 107.5, Total Fat: 0.6 g, Saturated Fat: 0.0 g, Carbs: 27.7 g, Sugars: 23.1 g, Protein: 1.8 g

Serves: 4

Ingredients:
2 lb Fresh, Ripe Peaches

Instructions:
- Rinse the peaches, halve them and remove the stones.
- Slice the halves into ¼-inch thick slices and place them on the dehydrator trays.
- Set the dehydrator to 135F / 57C and dry the peaches from 5 to 24 hours, depending on the thickness of the slices and how dry you want the peaches to be.
- When done, store in airtight containers and set aside.

Dehydrated Cantaloupe

Calories: 25, Total Fat: 0.3 g, Saturated Fat: 0.0 g, Carbs: 5.0 g, Sugars: 53 g, Protein: 0.5 g

Serves: 4

Ingredients:
1 Cantaloupe

Instructions:
- Halve the cantaloupe and remove the seeds.
- Cut the cantaloupe into thin slices, remove the skin and place on the dehydrator trays.
- Dehydrate at 135F / 57C for 10-12 hours or until dried.
- Store in airtight containers and set aside.

Banana Chips

Calories: 180.5, Total Fat: 0.7 g, Saturated Fat: 0.3 g, Carbs: 46.2 g, Sugars: 24.8 g, Protein: 2.2 g

Serves: 10

Ingredients:
½ cup Fresh Lemon Juice
20 Bananas

Instructions:
- Pour the juice into a shallow dish.
- Peel the bananas and cut them lengthwise into 1/8-inch thick slices. Alternatively, you can slice them into 1/8-inch thick rounds.
- As you work, add the banana slices to the dish with the lemon juice to soak for 5-10 minutes.
- Arrange the slices to the dehydrator trays and dry for about 24 hours at 135F / 57C. Check the bananas every 6 or so hours.
- When done, store in airtight containers and set aside.

Dehydrated Grapes

Calories: 96.9, Total Fat: 0.5 g, Saturated Fat: 0.5 g, Carbs: 25.0 g, Sugars: 23.4 g, Protein: 0.8 g

Serves: 4

Ingredients:
2 lbs Grapes
2 tsp Citric Acid

Instructions:
- Rinse the grapes, leave them in a colander to drain and discard the stems and any spoiled grapes, then bring a large pot with water to the boil and blanch the grapes for half a minute or until the skins start to crackle.
- Transfer to a pot filled with icy cold water and citric acid. Stir around for about 10 minutes and then drain.
- Arrange on the dehydrator trays and dry for 24 hours at 135F / 57C. Check the grapes every 2 hours, and if after 24 hours they are still moist, dry them for a couple of more hours.
- When done, allow the raisins to cool on the trays and then store in airtight containers.

Dried Mango

Calories: 184.1, Total Fat: 0.7 g, Saturated Fat: 0.2 g,
Carbs: 48.3 g, Sugars: 42.6 g, Protein: 1.3 g

Serves: 4

Ingredients:
¼ cup Lemon Juice
1 Tbsp Raw Honey
5 Ripe Mangoes

Instructions:
- Mix together the lemon juice and honey until the honey has dissolved.
- Peel the mangoes and slice them into thin strips.
- Coat the slices with the lemon and honey mixture and arrange on the dehydrator trays.
- Dehydrate at 135F / 57C for 10-12 hours, checking after 8 hours.
- When done, allow to cool and then store in airtight containers.

Dried Watermelon

Calories: 168.7, Total Fat: 0.7 g, Saturated Fat: 0.0 g, Carbs: 42.6 g, Sugars: 35.0 g, Protein: 3.4 g

Serves: 8

Ingredients:
1 Watermelon, medium-sized
Sea Salt, to taste

Instructions:
- Chop the watermelon into wedges and cut them into ¼-inch pieces.
- Place in a bowl, sprinkle with salt and toss to coat.
- Arrange the slices on dehydrator trays and dehydrate at 140F / 60C for about 11 hours or until the desired doneness.
- Allow to cool and store in airtight containers.

Dehydrated Apricots

Calories: 243.5, Total Fat: 1.6 g, Saturated Fat: 0.1 g, Carbs: 58.4 g, Sugars: 50.9 g, Protein: 5.7 g

Serves: 10

Ingredients:
1 gallon Water, for soaking
½ cup White Vinegar
½ cup Honey
1 cup Water
4 lb Apricots

Instructions:
- Combine the water and vinegar and soak the apricots for 10 minutes. Drain and rinse the fruits, slice in half and discard the stones.
- Mix together the honey and water, add the apricots and toss to coat. Allow to sit for 15 minutes so that the apricots soak the honey mixture.
- Arrange the apricot halves onto dehydrator trays and dehydrate at 135F / 57C for 9-12 hours.
- Allow to cool and store in airtight containers.

Dehydrated Avocado Chips

Calories: 288.8, Total Fat: 26.6 g, Saturated Fat: 3.7 g, Carbs: 15.0 g, Sugars: 0.5 g, Protein: 3.4 g

Serves: 4

Ingredients:
4 Avocados, halved and sliced into ¼-inch thick slices (not peeled)
¼ cup Fresh Cilantro, chopped
½ Lemon, juiced
¼ tsp Cayenne Pepper
¼ tsp Sea Salt

Instructions:
- Drizzle the avocado sliced with the lemon juice, peel them and arrange on your dehydrator trays.
- Sprinkle with the chopped cilantro, salt, and cayenne and dehydrate at 165F / 74C for 8-10 hours.
- Allow to cool and store in airtight containers.

Dehydrated Clementine

Calories: 87.5, Total Fat: 0.0 g, Saturated Fat: 0.0 g, Carbs: 22.5 g, Sugars: 17.5 g, Protein: 2.5 g

Serves: 4

Ingredients:
10 Clementine

Instructions:
- Rinse the clementine (do not peel them) and slice into thin slices. Arrange on your dehydrator trays and dehydrate at 135F / 57C for 12-14 hours, depending on the thickness of the slices.
- Allow to cool and store in airtight containers.

Dehydrated Figs

Calories: 111.0, Total Fat: 0.5 g, Saturated Fat: 0.1 g, Carbs: 28.8 g, Sugars: 24.4 g, Protein: 1.1 g

Serves: 6

Ingredients:
2 lb Fresh Ripe Figs

Instructions:

- Fill a large pot with water and bring it to the boil. Add the figs, blanch them for half a minute, take them out and immediately place in a pot filled with ice cold water.
- Arrange the figs on your dehydrator trays and dehydrate at 135F / 57C for 8-24 hours depending on the size of the figs.
- When the figs are dry but still chewy, remove them from the dehydrator, allow to cool and store in airtight containers.

Dehydrated Kiwi

Calories: 91.5, Total Fat: 0.7 g, Saturated Fat: 0.0 g, Carbs: 22.3 g, Sugars: 0.1 g, Protein: 1.5 g

Serves: 6

Ingredients:
2 lb Kiwis, peel

Instructions:
- Slice the kiwis into ¼-inch slices and arrange them on your dehydrator trays.
- Leave to dehydrate at 135F / 57C for about 6-12 hours until the slices are completely dried.
- Allow to cool and store in airtight containers.

CHAPTER 8: JERKY RECIPES

Sweet Heart Jerky

Calories: 157.5, Total Fat: 4.0 g, Saturated Fat: 1.2 g, Carbs: 4.3 g, Sugars: 4.2 g, Protein: 24.1 g

Serves: 6

Ingredients:
1 Beef Heart, frozen
½ cup Water
¾ cup Pineapple Juice
1 Tbsp Vinegar
2 Tbsp Fish Sauce
½ tsp Garlic Powder
1 tsp Garam Masala
¼ tsp White Pepper
¼ tsp Ground Ginger
¼ tsp Ground Cardamom
¼ tsp Ground Coriander

Instructions:
- One day before making the jerky, place the frozen heart into the freezer. Slice the heart into ¼-inch thick slices.
- Mix together the remaining ingredients and pour into a sealable container. Microwave for a minute and add the slices into the marinade. Seal the container and keep in the fridge for at least 4 hours.
- Dehydrate at 145F / 62C for 6 hours, rotating and flipping the trays.
- Allow to cool and store in airtight containers.

Salmon Jerky

Calories: 361.9, Total Fat: 7.4 g, Saturated Fat: 1.2 g, Carbs: 35.5 g, Sugars: 32.9 g, Protein: 45.3 g

Serves: 6

Ingredients:
2 lb Salmon, skin removed
1 cup Soy Sauce
1 Orange, zest and juice
1/4 cup Cracked Black Pepper
1 cup Brown Sugar
1/4 cup Mesquite Smoked Liquid Smoke
3 Tbsp Ground Black Pepper
3 Tbsp Sea Salt

Instructions:
- Slice the salmon into strips, place in a sealable container and set aside.
- Whisk together the soy sauce, orange juice, cracked black pepper, brown sugar, and liquid smoke. Pour the marinade over the salmon, seal and keep in the fridge for 12-24 hours to marinate.
- Pat dry the salmon, arrange on dehydrator trays and sprinkle with the orange zest, salt and pepper.
- Dehydrate at 155F / 70C for 5 hours. Allow to cool and store in airtight containers.

Chinese Pork Jerky

Calories: 533.1, Total Fat: 34.6 g, Saturated Fat: 12.9 g, Carbs: 10.0 g, Sugars: 10.0 g, Protein: 42.8 g

Serves: 6

Ingredients:
2 lb Ground Pork
2 Tbsp Shao Hsing Cooking Wine
1 Tbsp Dark Soy Sauce
1 Tbsp Fish Sauce
1 tsp Sesame Oil
½ tsp Ground Pepper
½ tsp Five-Spice Powder
2/3 cup Sugar

Instructions:
- Add the ingredients to a large bowl and mix to combine. Cover and keep in the fridge for at least 4 hours.
- Line dehydrator trays with parchment paper and spread the mixture into thin layers. Cover with parchment paper and gently press to even out and smoothen the meat strips.
- Dehydrate at 145F / 62C for 6 hours. Flip and dehydrate for a few more hours until dried.
- Allow to cool and store in airtight containers.

Goose Jerky

Calories: 556.5, Total Fat: 50.4 g, Saturated Fat: 14.7 g, Carbs: 5.3 g, Sugars: 9.7 g, Protein: 23. g

Serves: 10

Ingredients:
3 lb Goose Breast Meat, skin and fat removed
1/4 cup Worcestershire Sauce
2 cup Water
1 tsp Garlic Powder
2 Tbsp Kosher Salt
3 Tbsp Brown Sugar
1 tsp Dried Thyme
1 tsp Cayenne

Instructions:
- Slice the meat into strips (approx. ¼-inch thick) and set aside.
- Combine the remaining ingredients in a bowl, add the meat and gently massage it to coat it evenly.
- Transfer the meat together with the marinade into a sealable bag and place in the fridge for 24-72 hours.
- Pat dry the meat and arrange on dehydrator trays. Dehydrate at 140F /60C for 6-8 hours.
- Allow to cool and store in airtight containers.

Sriracha Tofu Jerky

Calories: 87.3, Total Fat: 5.2 g, Saturated Fat: 1.1 g, Carbs: 2.1 g, Sugars: 0.7 g, Protein: 10.2 g

Serves: 4

Ingredients:
1/2 lb Extra Firm Tofu
1/2 tsp Liquid Smoke
1/4 tsp Garlic Powder
2 Tbsp Soy Sauce
2 tsp Sriracha

Instructions:
- Drain the tofu and slice into ¼-inch thick slices.
- Mix together the remaining ingredients and brush the tofu slices on both sides.
- Arrange on dehydrator trays and dehydrate at 135F /57C for 8-10 hours or until dry.
- Allow to cool and store in airtight containers.

Venison Jerky

Calories: 265.6, Total Fat: 4.0 g, Saturated Fat: 1.5 g, Carbs: 2.9 g, Sugars: 2.2 g, Protein: 51.0 g

Serves: 6

Ingredients:
2 lb Venison Steak, fat removed
¼ cup Worcestershire Sauce
¼ cup Soy Sauce
1½ tsp Liquid Smoke
1 tsp Onion Powder
½ tsp Garlic Powder
½ tsp Crushed Garlic
½ tsp Smoked Pepper
¼ tsp Chili Powder
1 Tbsp Ground Coriander
½ tsp Cracked Pepper
1 tsp Sea Salt

Instructions:
- Slice the meat into thin slices and place in a sealable bag.
- Whisk together the remaining ingredients and pour into the bag with the meat. Toss to coat the meat and keep in the fridge for 24-48 hours to marinate. Toss a few times during this time.

- Pat dry the meat and arrange on dehydrator trays. Dehydrate at 150F / 65C for 4-8 hours depending on the thickness of the strips.
- Allow to cool and store in airtight containers.

Simple Deer Jerky

Calories: 270, Total Fat: 5.3 g, Saturated Fat: 2.1 g, Carbs: 1 g, Sugars: 0.2 g, Protein: 51.2 g

Serves: 6

Ingredients:

2 lb Deer Roast, Steak, or Loin
2 Tbsp Liquid Smoke
1/3 cup Soy Sauce
1/2 cup Water
1 tsp Sea Salt
¼ tsp Black Pepper
Cayenne Pepper, to taste

Instructions:

- Slice the meat into thin slices removing fat and place in a sealable bag.
- Mix together the remaining ingredients, pour into the bag with the meat and toss to coat. Keep in the fridge overnight to marinate.
- Pat dry the meat strips and arrange them on dehydrator trays. Dehydrate at 150F / 65C for 6-8 hours depending on the thickness of the slices. Cool and store in airtight containers.

Teriyaki Chicken Jerky

Calories: 204.2, Total Fat: 6 g, Saturated Fat: 2.2 g, Carbs: 0 g, Sugars: 0.1 g, Protein: 36.5 g

Serves: 6

Ingredients:
4 Boneless Chicken Breast Halves, skin removed
1/4 tsp Red Pepper Flakes
½ cup Teriyaki Sauce

Instructions:
- Slice the chicken into ¼-inch thick strips and place in a sealable bag.
- Add the sauce and red pepper flakes and toss to coat. Refrigerate for an hour to marinate.
- Pat dry, arrange on dehydrator trays and dry at 150F / 60C for 5-7 hours.
- Allow to cool and store in airtight container.

Cauliflower Jerky

Calories: 110.3, Total Fat: 7.0 g, Saturated Fat: 10 g, Carbs: 10.1 g, Sugars: 0.1 g, Protein: 5.0 g

Serves: 4

Ingredients:
1/4 cup + 2 Tbsp Raw Tahini
1 Tbsp Nutritional Yeast
1 Tbsp Apple Cider Vinegar
1-4 tsp Sriracha
1/4 cup Vegetable Broth, plus more if needed
1/2 tsp Liquid Smoke
1/4 tsp Sea Salt
1 head of Cauliflower, broken into small florets

Instructions:
- Whisk together the ingredients except the cauliflower and salt. Add the cauliflower florets and gently stir to coat.
- Arrange the florets onto dehydrator trays, sprinkle with salt and dehydrate at 130F / 54C for 12-14 hours.
- Allow to cool and store in airtight containers.

Basic Beef Jerky

Calories: 353.0, Total Fat: 13.3 g, Saturated Fat: 5.2 g, Carbs: 4.0 g, Sugars: 0.1 g, Protein: 50.7 g

Serves: 6

Ingredients:
2 lb Lean Beef Meat

Ingredients for the marinade:
2 Tbsp Worcestershire Sauce
1/4 cup Balsamic Vinegar
1/4 cup Water
1 Tbsp Dried Minced Onion
4 Garlic Cloves, crushed
1 Tbsp Sea Salt
1 Tbsp Black Pepper

Instructions:
- Start preparing the meat by trimming off any large portions of fat. Place the meat in the freezer for about 5-10 minutes.
- Slice the meat in strips of the desired size (the meat will shrink for about 2/3 of its starting size).
- To prepare the marinade:
- Mix together the ingredients and pour them into a sealable bag, add the meat, seal and make shake gently to coat the meat with the marinade. Place in

the fridge and leave to marinate for at least 4 but not more than 24 hours.

- Heat your oven to 392F / 200C, arrange the meat strips on the racks and cook for an hour.
- Take the meat out of the oven and arrange it on the dehydrator rack. Dehydrate at 135F / 57C for at least 10 hours until the desired doneness.
- When done, remove and leave to cool on paper towels. Store in airtight containers.

Trout Jerky

Calories: 33, Total Fat: 14.6 g, Saturated Fat: 0 g, Carbs: 1.2 g, Sugars: 0.3 g, Protein: 58.3 g

Serves: 4

Ingredients:
1/4 cup Soy Sauce
1 tsp Olive Oil
1/2 tsp Black Pepper
1 Tbsp Brown Sugar
1 tsp Minced Garlic
1 lb Trout Fillets, cut into 1-inch wide strips lengthwise

Instructions:
- Whisk together all the ingredients (except the fish) in a pot and heat on low. When the sugar has dissolved, remove the pot from the heat and leave to cool.
- Place the fish fillets into a sealable bag and pour in the marinade. Seal, toss to coat and keep in the fridge for 4 hours.
- Take out the fish, pat dry and arrange on dehydrator trays. Dehydrate at 135F / 57C for 6-8 hours or until desired doneness. Allow to cool and store in sealed plastic bags.

Turkey Jerky

Calories: 214.4, Total Fat: 4.0 g, Saturated Fat: 1.3 g, Carbs: 4.7 g, Sugars: 4.2 g, Protein: 37.6 g

Serves: 4

Ingredients:
2 Tbsp Soy Sauce
1 Tbsp Liquid Smoke
1/3 cup Worcestershire Sauce
1/4 tsp Tabasco Sauce
2 tsp Garlic Powder
1 Tbsp Onion Powder
2 tsp Brown Sugar
1 tsp Kosher Salt
1 lb Turkey Meat, thinly sliced

Instructions:
- Whisk together the soy sauce, liquid smoke, sauces, garlic and onion powder, sugar, and kosher salt and pour the mixture into a scalable bag.
- Add the turkey slices, seal and toss to coat. Keep in the fridge for up to 24 hours to marinate.
- Take out the turkey strips, pat dry them and arrange on your dehydrator trays. Dehydrate at 135F / 57C for 8-10 hours depending on the thickness of the slices.
- Allow to cool and store in airtight container.

Made in the USA
Middletown, DE
27 December 2017